T0243246

South Side of
a Kinless River

South Side of a
Kinless
River

Marilyn Dumont

Brick Books

Library and Archives Canada Cataloguing in Publication

Title: South side of a kinless river / Marilyn Dumont.
Names: Dumont, Marilyn, 1955- author.
Description: Includes some text in Cree.
Identifiers: Canadiana (print) 20240401050 | Canadiana (ebook) 20240401069 |
ISBN 9781771316316 (softcover) | ISBN 9781771316323 (EPUB) | ISBN 9781771316330 (PDF)
Subjects: LCGFT: Poetry.
Classification: LCC PS8557.U53633 S68 2024 | DDC C811/.54—dc23

Copyright © Marilyn Dumont, 2024

We gratefully acknowledge the Canada Council for the Arts, the Government of Canada through
the Canada Book Fund, and the Ontario Arts Council and the Government of Ontario for their
support of our publishing program.

Edited by Katherena Vermette.
Cover image by Krista Leddy:
    Two Teacups, 2024 (glass beads, gold and copper plated glass beads, wool).
Author photo by Amanda Yakem.
The book is set in Minion Pro.
Design by Marijke Friesen.

Brick Books
487 King St. W.
Kingston, ON
K7L 2X7
www.brickbooks.ca

Though much of the work of Brick Books takes place on the ancestral lands of the Anishinaabeg,
Haudenosaunee, Huron-Wendat, and Mississaugas of the Credit peoples, our editors, authors,
and readers from many backgrounds are situated from coast to coast to coast in Canada on the
traditional and unceded territories of over six hundred nations who have cared for Turtle Island
from time immemorial. While living and working on these lands, we are committed to hearing
and returning the rightful imaginative space to the poetries, songs, and stories that have been
untold, under-told, wrongly told, and suppressed through colonization.

Dedicated to all my relatives who struggled to make space
for those who came after them.

CONTENTS

Throwing the language dice

Flour-sack dresses billow in the wind

misāskwatōmina

This settlement began split by a river
a blue ribbon
down the middle
red rose tea on both banks
North side – stovepipe hats
South side – octopus bags

                    Northside company men and Michif wives
                    Southside pāhpāscēs and halfbreeds

Rowand fathers my cāpān

François Dufresne
my mother's kin almost
lost to me

Colonialism is an absence that widens
a flood of Puritanism
a downpour of intolerance
The knife of industry
severs kin

Riverbed stratified

Light the story of Margaret, Marie, Madeline
deemed immaterial, not unusual
but my mother's kin is missing
Missing kin turn

                    vague
                    turn forgotten

While women hold the frame
men look through
shadow women
receding in the balsam and shrub bush
surveyors, guides, river lots

The south side of the stockade
faded English flag flapping; this is the manitow Empire
river lot system   a raft reproducing the race
misāskwatōmina – fruit of the tree of many branches   Saskatoons
Northwest Half-Breed Scrip did not civilize any more than river chemistry
produced sovereignty   Pack horses meander through beaked hazelnut
Noblemen, squirrels harvesting chokecherries
The Dominion Telegraph forging through coarse grasses
Sediment-tilling Grey Nuns   colonize, too
renaming John Walter's Ferry
a braided river   Downstream, beaver plow with Red River carts
impersonate river channels scattering trees
Company coat of arms, black suits with brass buttons
Erosion is the point of emergence

A nation of Indigenous midwives delivered this country

Brown bent women
singing water-circles
rain-suckling
minnow-threading

babies licked to sleep swinging
threading
through wēwēpison

awāsisak
flannel-wrapped cradle
suspended between long ropes
strung corner to corner

within easy reach of a tired brown hand
lulling awāsis to sleep

Dark women circle
brooding litters
women with strong minds
and swings across their beds
suckle minnows to sleep
through water veins

Water-webbed
suckled minnows threading
through swoop-fluid diving
brown hands massaging
the belly of the motherland
steeping wild raspberry tea
for the coming labour

Memory is a cemetery

I've visited once or twice, white
ubiquitous and the set aside
Everywhere underfoot ...
—Charles Wright

Ubiquitous walks through me regularly
down streets named Whyte, Grierson, or Jasper
reiterating my absence

This bluff overlooking the kisiskāciwani-sīpiy was envisioned
as brickworks, smokestacks, and glass mills
When amiskwaciy-wāskahikan floated in prairie grass
so high you used a compass to cross it
after a two-month cart ride from Winnipeg

When Kwarakwante, Callihoo, pāhpāscēs, Bobtail, and atāhkakohp gathered
river flats rocks rasped their stories
long before Oliver, Grierson, or Strathcona – their names barbed-wire reminders
sewn to the Imperial centre, ignoring any glimpse of Lapotac,
the fort's hunter flinting chert for deer-hunting arrows
before this city constructed a myth of steel bridges, concrete stories of
"settlement" and "pioneers"

Ubiquitous rarely owns the brown memory of a Métis great-grandmother, a
Cree Iroquois Mohawk Nakoda or Blackfoot cāpān, the Carlton-trail-cart-
driving relatives, the third cousin twice removed in St. Albert, the HBC
paymaster, or the Orkney York boat-building side of the family

Ubiquitous knows that exile is space without language to speak of it
that alienation is a wall only you can see

Indigenous midwives

When she was born   the universe, hers
was born, was born the universe
the universe was born in her water

giant, bronze, and Indigenous

Paired, the moon and earth
This was her galaxy
She was a shooting star
Comets clustered 'round her copper breasts and belly
                  some suckling
                      some craving

The black whetstone
of her long hair
heats in the sun

ignites awe

Her spiral arms   and
cosmic expansion
interstellar contractions
popping fur trade citizens through every
window and
settler-wives
admit their newborn
from the bronzed arms
of Indigenous midwives
who are goaded out of town –
because if you can see her, she's not Indigenous

Lizette, "Shining Star"

There is no surviving image of you
not visible to the naked eye
                              but spun to life
                                    by a silken thread
drawn down a dream
through a prologue
to seven sisters and a
bearded ohkomimāw
hairy, long-legged
                    orb-spinning
                                      chain-smoking
kōhkom spider
                    a rollie glued to her lip
                    hankie pushed up her sleeve
Her labour – the mother craft
releasing life-threads
linking cosmic expansion
accumulating neon sisters, the auroras
extended through starlight and wavelength
orbiting the Gwynne Channel
its ice faults, glacial splits
calving off and
draining Lake Edmonton

to a flat earth listing heavy
fearful settlers and
white-melting-skinned women
who required midwives and medicine

to no surviving image of you, Lizette
your face a hole in the sun of this recorded empire
of men engraving their names everywhere
while nameless
strong-faced women
of no consequence
helped them survive

I am left with questions, Lizette:
Did you stoke your clay pipe after sex
filled with red willow and kinikinik
or did you recite your rosary and pray?

Did your black braids glisten in the rain?

Reviving a petrified history

Surely, I am as visible as that balsam on the edge of this river

this city I live in I built with bones / and mortared with marrow of nēhiyawiskwēw

stratification dating

when Indigenous women elevate settler men to prominence

like my great-great-grandfather, cāpān, Hudson's Bay Factor, Rowand

scrambling eggs for colonial mornings

breaking

fast

separating the yolk in search of the first white baby born in Rupertsland

delivered by an Indigenous midwife

    – turns out Riel's grandmother

wasn't the first woman to deliver a mōniyāw

but she conceived a clan that would set a prairie fire

Governor Simpson

... when the nights turned cold, he was not quite as alone
as his journals might indicate.
—James Raffan

His title and generous libido
took him to the chill of a foreign place and people
His desire for Indigenous women
caught him with his palisades down
unfurling his puritan corkscrew
to eight Indigenous women and thirteen babies

His inclination for Cree-Métis women's silken breasts
warming brown against his sin
their smell of woodsmoke
his own stench of loneliness and fear
inside her rabbit-fur blankets
comforting but haunting his struggle –

the struggle within his belted pinstriped pants
but inevitable return to his "washer woman"
brown wives and daughters offered to
the "randy Scotsman"

who is salt-pocked with guilt and shame
Eight "bits of brown"
and thirteen children later
he fears talk might extend his reputation far beyond
the worst philandering before him
and pines for a lighter-skinned woman
perhaps someone British

who will salvage his rusting hull
and the hubris of noblemen
projecting themselves upon a place
erecting a seedling nation in the image of themselves
first, through the children of trade

He enters the burnt-wood territory
seeds himself
over and over
out of lust, out of greed
He feeds
himself, seeds himself into being in
this place with big animals, relentless weather, and unpredictable Indians
or worse – the Métis half known, half-trusted

But Sir George can't keep his hands off the
brown earth force of Indigenous women

Sir George, who, instead of rejoicing with her
is dragged down by Puritan notions of dowsing
the human need for sex
transcending the weaker vessel
sin and all dark
But he relents time after time to the perfect white smile
of a brown woman who has just fed her babies
the richest meal they ever had from her breast

Betsy Brass and Shining Star were sisters

Betsy didn't reflect
she shone copper
in her image
her horses wild in the field
so ablaze with dream
their giant heads and proud horse-collars
lifting, emboldened by ascension
fetlocks lofting in their air-strides
wrestling airborne jingling tack and hooves sculling
over clerks passed out in their bunkhouses
afraid and green to this prairie

While Lizette glowed bronze
blue-black hair and cinnamon skin
she pulled babies through her belly button and interstellar arms
A herder of star-sisters and horses
calculator of made beaver and barley
Lac Ste. Anne whitefish
North Saskatchewan sturgeon
Pemmican and timid clerks
and a ripe dowry
for a "randy" Scotsman

Reaping women

All were killed
except nine women
away gathering turnips
twisting tethered purple heads
from the amniotic sweet woodiness
bridled in their long white roots

All but nine women
away gathering taproots
were killed by redcoats, their husbands' heads
purple-wound in grass
sacks dropped to the earth
kin dead in doorways, at tables, in beds
limbs strewn, mutilated

Nine women's hands
lifting bodies
once gathering turnips
now braiding hair
twisting flying-bright colours
into tobacco ties for burning

Now, robing men in moose hides
boys in deer hide

skin-held
        resting
                wrapped

canoes ready for a smoky sky
made ready by women's hands

Faults of motherhood

New spruce shoots and moss breath
an absence of mistakes in motherhood
would make us all holy

Margaret Harriott on horseback through the Rockies
star-flowered days through nodding trillium
her young daughter and son
needy limbs competing for her
Mind unlatched, uncapped
her long train of faults dragging behind her
she covets her infant at night
sleeps bear-heavy in hibernation
nuzzles his scent close

but, through night terror, uncovers him
limp, lifeless
under her weight
her large body squeezing
the light out of him
as she dreamt of life
Panicked
she prays for any
small wind
to blow back into him
his tiny corpse a stone weight in her bed, now

Distraught, she flees
careening through the rough spruce and black fir
her feet bare and bleeding, catching on torment
her night shirt shredding dead leaves and branches

her legs chokecherry stained and scratched
her breasts moulting
remembering his smell, his suckling sour mouth
To face herself
heartwood would be pierced
acts like hers – are unspeakable violations
a caveat on motherhood
fused with infanticide
the fault of motherhood
careening through the dark wood
being swallowed by what accidents could deliver

Rowand's folly

The root cellar of her heart gave way the day he went missing; she fevered and fretted over this rotund white stranger who might be a fine country match; she felt his eyes tracing the dotted line of her ghosted country where her ancestors' travois traced maps. When she spotted him, small crumpled dot on the broken-leg prairie, his reflection in her eyes was bigger than he'd dreamt. He saw a river of beaver pelts stretching down the North Saskatchewan brought by her relatives, the pelts shiny and thick, baled for loading into York Boats; saw men wearing sashes, smoking pipes, leaning their lives into the silt and shifting sand of the North Saskatchewan; he saw her steeping scrapped hides in alder bark; he saw Burnt-Wood people, camps and quarries, men flaking chert into arrowheads and cutting tools; he saw women in moccasins, short leggings, and wrap-around kilts picking saskatoons for pounding into the dust of buffalo meat; he saw a fort, his own folly, and settlers brought by the giant black horse.

One Pound One, Big Mountain, Iron Shirt

for Louise Umfreville

I have crossed this river countless times, she thought, her unchained self
slipping into updrafts and down-turning dreams; name it an itch or an urge;
she reached out, her mind in search of a young clerk, his horse returned
without him. Who knows what this otipēyimisow woman camped on the
tabled North Saskatchewan River flats envisioned when the rotund Rowand
said, "tānisi" to her fat dowry of horses? He alone went hunting that day,
the horse reared, whipping its backbone into a figure eight, before throwing
his Big Mountain – 300lbs, too much for any dumb limb – onto the prairie.
His leg snapping under the weight of his ambition to rise from good clerk to
Czar of the Prairies – where she'd eventually take him – her conveyor belt of
relatives delivering pelts right to his front door. Why search for Big Mountain,
this Iron Shirt? This foreign man who could outwork 'n outswear any man
she'd known. What picture of herself did she see in him that day she emerged
from her tent to meet his eyes? The days when a fur trade monopoly made
both their choices. What seduced her? Him? Or his horse?

Victoria's jig

Victoria Calihoo enters a jigging contest on her hundredth birthday
lining up with girls in stiff crinolines and women with child-rearing legs
She in high-top moccasins, patched dress, and hide-skinning muscle
takes the dance floor
the attention of onlookers converging
on her tiny gray frame alone at the centre
her toes at attention, waiting to spring
to the fiddler's bow, swept along
strumming guitar stitching her feet to strings bending,
the hem of her dress bouncing
audience gasping at her feet, exacting swift step changes
Weightless and nimble, she skim-shuffles in the fiddler's trance
her young face shining through her smile, bouncing off the surprised
faces of the child-rearing women, the deflated crinolines of girls leaning in
disappointment
as Victoria takes first place

Victoria Belcourt's player piano

Levers and pneumatic pedals
strike crescendos, diminuendos, and tempo
drive slats an' pegs to bellow
waltz ever into high-hat
rafters echolocate beams
then stall
        Dives in a murmuration of starlings
mesmer-matched wings
swooping and plunging
fall
in shards of dried moose meat dropping
                flopping into the laps of Victoria's guests
who gleefully stuff their pockets and
bulging groundhog cheeks

But before the sweet dried meat has stopped raining
shingles turn, and Victoria's pumping foot-treadle
ignites bass and treble
her guests flock to the dance floor
in foxtrot and polka
while Victoria ruminates
handy with a keyboard and chiselled face

The wire

At one hundred and one, Victoria Belcourt Callihoo
tested her Cree on pīwāpiskwēyāpiy,
"kinēhiyawān cī?"
her pronunciation echo-circling
small-winging her words
barn sparrows and wasps
syllables whistling amiskwaciy-wāskahikan, wītaskīwin, and maskwacīs
through the thin black lines back
to Victoria's ear and a plump smile confirming
that the white man's black stick, the long black line –
pīwāpiskwēyāpiy – works

Red River cart written all over it

> *Each year the dead grow less dead, and nudge*
> *Close to the surface of all things.*
> *They start to remember the silence that brought them there.*
> —Charlies Wright, from "Homage to Paul Cezanne"

Dust-eroded paths admit their bones
along
her banks engraved
with cartwheel runnels
of the first highway

Red-River-cart trails
sew this valley
   southside Strathcona
     northside Jasper
      amiskwaciy-wāskahikan set
along a chain of settlements
trade hubs and seasonal storylines
all drain back into kisiskāciwani-sīpiy

Listen
there may be stories
left near the shore
stones or blue chipped beads
still
silt-silent
below the bellowing mōniyāwak stories
silt-silent nest of roads
spokes in a wheel spreading
the rutted cart trails

along the Pembina to the Peace
these Rossdale Flats have
Red River cart written all over it

Flat rocks rasp their stories

All my archival relations'

faces are disquieting
solemn and infinitely lonely
prisoners of alphabetical order and silence

Calumet-smoking, Cree-speaking halfbreeds
        elude lost kin

The "country way" only identified "halfbreeds" and "Indian women"
Nomenclature was in short supply, apparently
               and life measured in ways that never amounted to much
a cold life captive in an archive
is hard to light
the heartwood dark

I imagine my cāpān,
François Dufresne Jr,
hostage at Frog Lake
born in a time when cowboys were Indian or Black

biological son of Chief Factor Rowand and Margaret Mondion,
Iroquois country wife,
raised as the son of a Frenchman, Edouard François Dufresne in Fort Pitt

I come from a family of interpreters and ventriloquists
our eyes tattooed kinscapes
over the light tables and micro-fiche
stumbling along half-lit paths to ourselves

A name, a date, a face, a few facts might lead to a life
but lives like facts are forgotten

a family tree reduced to fallen timber
erasing visible tracks back to ourselves

Windblown faces petition me
Stories – I would follow anywhere

So, perhaps there is life among the sepia photographs
moth-eaten sashes
the few facts are maps back

We're the half kin

          āpihtawikosisān – half son of
the Cree
who say we're half empty
while settlers see us half-full

Half-skinned, half-measured
              while measured more than most
Half human, half devil
      treacherous halves   threaten to split
half turn on the whole
My relatives – interpreters and ventriloquists
cāpān and nimosōmipan
both conjuring English from Cree
for Indian Agents
who saw the world as notched pronouns
of ownership, territory, and trade

cāpān and nimosōmipan
ventriloquists of English
Half speaking, half acting
speech-acting the English
throwing the dice of language on the table
hoping for it to roll in favour of the Cree signatories

Moorings

When the heavy horses loosened the one-room schoolhouse from its moorings
did you lean into that room where your children's lives might sprout, or
recall your own brief time in a classroom before following your father to work?

When you chose the schoolhouse
did you imagine your ten kids sitting at attention before a teacher at the
blackboard?
Did you hear the echo of her reciting the English alphabet
the pointer striking the chalkboard in unison
with the enunciation of the Roman orthography?

A for "Ambrose"? B for "brown-skinned"? C for "Cree"?
Sounds stinging your ears to attention

Did you see your children writing their names in fluid strokes
alongside your signature rehearsed and jagged?
Your hands more practised at steadying a chainsaw
your size-thirteen fingers dwarfing any blunt pencil

Did you see them handing in their assignments
walking to the blackboard without fear
reading aloud
their hands shooting up to answer first?

A for "Ambrose"?
B for "brown-skinned boy"?
C for "Cree"?
The English still stinging your ear

Did you imagine them speaking perfect English?
Their Cree wiped from the chalkboard

Did you imagine transporting a colonial world across the prairie for us?

My mother's story is

blurred –
the lines to her heartkin
were passed over
clouding the maternal lines to kin, she
tried to share, but the grand
male narrative annexed her life
parceled it into
to the next male relative
in a mother's-life-comes-last
kinda way

Eyes like punched-out diamonds
haul me back in
if I turn away from
the faded kin

In my brother's face
I see my cāpān
and – like a great-granddaughter with
a life – failed to notice
I want to be held in the
tobacco smoke and wool twill
of your embrace, cāpān

Your windblown face haunts questions
without answers
Blank minded, I look into my brother's face, and I see you –
but you never lived to see us

Details lost except
angles of cheekbones and crow's feet surrounding your eyes
nikāwiy told me you wrote poetry
the rest of your life – I imagine
long-sleeved shirts with garters
tented eyelids in wire-rimmed glasses
solemn-faced
with Homburg hats and
brass-buttoned people who owned themselves

I come sounding after

nīsta mīna   nīsta mīna
stamina
nīsta mīna

sweet syllables recalled
summoned from a dormant motherly shoot
ripening its way to
larynx strung to my sound-belly
aural memory loosening
a sound root
stretched over dusty tongue and ear
pull together

        no sound alone
union of larynx and lips
sounding our nēhiyaw-bodysong
through our moose stew and bangs
our dry meat and baked bannock
our bone marrow soup

I come sounding after
nikāwiy, nōhtāwiy
and some swimming of a brother's laugh splashing my face

I come sounding after
āniski-ohtāwīmāw
nōhkom

nīsta mīna

nitōn
nistikwān

this tongue loosens, delights
lights   enlightens
aural memory arriving home
from a long time ago:
nikāwiy thank you for birthing me
nōhtāwiy, thank you for never leaving me

a sound alone

nīsta mīna comes from you both
recalling sound sliver
nīsta mīna my mother combs my hair
my father tickles my feet
nīsta mīna, my brother teases me
nīsta mīna they call me back through kin vibrations
faces envelope me in the electric energy of affinity
opening the front door
pīhtikwē

I am a ventriloquist of my parents, nōhkom, cāpān

my lips, tongue, larynx
thread sound of the same mother tongue
stringing nīsta mīna

I'm tired
nīsta mīna

I'm hungry
nīsta mīna

I am lonely for your sounds

Lac Ste. Anne

Through bead, she is nimāmā
Through thread, she is nōhkom
Through needle, she is stitched   to l'historie

Through bead, she is pressed to cloth
each plea a bead to Saint Anne
nōhkominān, who never turns away
grandmother, who provides

Through seed she worries the beads
thumb-polished thoughts
cool, slick river stones, now

Each bead a prayer clasped to bead-prayer, miyo-Saint Anne
a thread pulling through each seed
holding bead of the rosary
hard seed black
suspended on linen cord
bundled in a shirt pocket
or dusty suit jacket
bright kerchiefs framing weathered faces
scramble of gravel church floor
rattle of birds in the arbor arms
shuffling coughs, crying children, Cree or Latin
spilling from the priest's mouth
riding above it all
a whole world for a week
suspended in Cree hymns

The ground spoke of you, Timothée

Rock face   cut bank   coulee   cliff

drop   transfer rift   reign

Born on the eclipse of the Rupertsland transfer
shifting continental reins
for a blind halfbreed craving land
on the poker table of governance
between church and state
Betrayal leeches out
the church walls
of St. Paul des Métis
runs down the wall stained in deceit like piss

The halfbreeds, church bait
for those obsessed with holiness and ascension
and turning perfectly good halfbreeds
into mōniyāwak

until we burn the school down
and become gravel in Father Therrien's shoe

so when ground spoke
and startled geese shot up from the lake

the ground stopped listening

Throwing the language dice

If Cree; If Water

> *If the water, everywhere, and if she*
> *is. If ghosts, like water, like if all*
> *rivers and oceans and rains are one*
> *ghost, surrounding and throughout.*
> —CJ Evans, from "Elegy in Limestone"

If nipiy is   if she is not   praised
if we are water   mostly we must
regard her   the fluid one   if she is
and if she   and if we   are one

nipiy

Water, is taught by thirst.
Land – by the Oceans passed.
Transport – by throe –
Peace – by its battles told –
Love, by Memorial Mold –
Birds, by the Snow.
—Emily Dickinson, 135

If our gratitude dries parched, we think nothing of   water
If our tongues shrink, we think of nothing   but water
of water, nothing of water – our foresight   shortened
dry, memory of   these-dry-days
Thirst is to recall water, call back self
relief in dry season
maskihkīwāpoy   its ebb and flow
wave together   call water   clear
call water   cold
call water   fast
call water   clean
call water   medicine
mint or Labrador steeped
from earth to vessel to table
vessel to vessel   poured   out
poured through

Bred

Bread bannock   dough   ingredients   gather in one place   Five Roses
salt, soda, water – the leavening   soda water – the agent   rises
salt-crystals glint   gather in one place   the biggest bowl   flour
salt, soda, water   in one place   at one time   measured by eye
in palm-cupped hands
flour-bag collar open at attention
hands plunging   ground wheat-heads   smooth weightless powder
cereal-brown dust   fingers   slipping silken   flour-air memory
salt, soda, water   kneaded   soft   elastic   dough
gathers in one place
the agents   the measured   the cupped   the leavened   the kneaded

Bread-bone

We are marrow bone, bred, held by water
bread-bone   marrow-berries
marrow dust   we are mortal marrow
a dusty union   crushed
ground into meat dust – made   pemmican

Is la bang le pain?

We are bone and bred
bone marrow et le beignet

                 boulet ēkwa beignet
                 bullets and bangs
A savoury sizzling doughnut   a cast-iron fry pan
la bang floating, crispy
crunchy frybread draining
impressing itself on empty egg cartons
before it's slathered with butter and jam or
honey from our mouths   bees swarm, berries sprout out from hair
while our flour-sack dresses billow in the wind

Deer life and death

"pē-mīciso!" meant supper meant elbow-to-elbow table-soup-
manners   reaching for thick slabs of baked bannock 'n butter 'n savoury
gravy of moose or deer sautéed in fat   meant browning and drippings meant
deer   tracks on our kitchen table as they pranced through us   the padded
sound of hooves drumming through   trotting out our inspired bellies
full now of deer life and death

Kinscape

Land hearthless
        hearthless life
land   landless   without
landlocked   hearthless
relatives   scatter
members disappear   dissolve without land-self to hold kin
        cāpān here
            nōhkom there
Métis line-threads   extend   families fray
divide like river-lots into rebellion and road allowance
hearts fray   hearth broken   without   home-
land without
scatter   separate   fragment kin   kinship
kin can't kin can't ship on   landlocked   hearthless
land   landless without   landlocked without
land   hearth   gone

I hold neither

land nor language
of my kin

nor speak
the language of my land

I tried apprehending the horizon
while confiscating a plot of land
measured my little motherland
threw down some stakes, and finally
inflicted statehood

My kingdom was my "two-eyed seeing"
My crown for solid ground
No more Métis
river lots or road allowance

This time, it's going to be land and language for all
Ground spoke Métis

It debated who was little *m* and who was *M* …
and debated

Just know that pairs are stuck together, and half is half
is full stop

For the ones not here

If you are where you are, then where
are those who are not here? Not Here.
—Natalie Diaz, from "Manhattan Is a Lenape Word"

My kin left no storied

                landlines to be read

fewer words and maps for we

                  yet inherited

                      landless

                          we who have not had

from those who are not here

Those who are not
fell through

           this talking land's throat

                      crosscut

not hearing   not holding

stories
that were not
to be carried

our fire starters
all left behind

Hear and hold
the stories
that were not
supposed to be

The colonial gaze

> *every language, even yours,*
> *is a partial map of the world*
> —Kei Miller, from "xx. in which the cartographer tells off the
> rastaman" in *The Cartographer Tries to Map a Way to Zion*

The colonial gaze   deserves a pair of thick glasses
generic black frames and heavy lenses correcting
tunnel vision: the blindness outside
its own centering

Think outside the Empire

Erase the whiteboard of:
        to discover: to pretend it's uninhabited
Verbs in the infinitive:
        to colonize: to enter someone's house and start renting the rooms
The colonial present:
        to civilize: to repeatedly construct the imaginary abject savage

I am starved for language that doesn't erode
doesn't sand away
swift syllables of gone

terra nullius

the haze
the gauze
leaning on brittle tropes
zealous phantoms

enter the ghosts that never leave the table
their gluttonous colony

Spitz

Some spit
stinking seed-thoughts

from a fruit bowl of
bruised colonial mislabelling
identity markers
and veiled co-constructions of vanishing Michif

Words slung around
a mail sorting room
of cut-kin
stinging
smell the blood
cut-kin

The erased, the rubbed out
sandpapered bones of "so-called" relations

Some people are free to mouth words, while some people suffer
barely survive them

Words: sometimes from under them crawl
the dark undersides of denotations
Relational platitudes
are swept up and thrown
in the dustbin of dreamt-up terms for Indigenous

"Sorry" doesn't reconcile anymore

"Sorry" doesn't quiver a forgiving bone in my Métis roots
sunflower-seed-sorries
relational contritions

"Sorry" no longer reconciles

mihcēto-pīkiskwēwak

We speak many languages
manifest unrecognizable shapes, sizes, and skin colours
We are not singularly visible
to the colonially challenged
who desire recognizable Indians

We speak Michif, Cree, Anishinaabe, Nakoda, Dene

We are born with
many phenotypes
Some of us
resemble
Others don't
Not a prototype of Louis
who was challenged for not looking Indigenous enough
Frequently there is no distinction
apart
from our FN relatives
but the colonial regime
desires a slow dissolve
into the next faded white glasses

disappearing us again
Others disappear us
as disowned kin
We are an addendum – sometimes added
Others re/collect us, barely

We are a watermark
a ghost image applied to the idea of Indigenous
the Métis: absently present
misperceived in between
We are followed by a false concept of purity
which we trouble

Are we the āpihtawikosisānak: the half sons of Cree ?

Or the otipēyimisowak: the people who own themselves?

NOTES

Reviving a petrified history: The italicized phrase is from Gwendolyn MacEwan's "The Garden of Square Roots: An Autobiography" in *Magic Animals: Selected Poems Old and New* (Macmillan Canada, 1974). Some details in the poem were found in D.R.King's *Alberta Archaeology: A Handbook for Amateurs* (The High River Times, 1968).

Governor Simpson: The epigraph is from James Raffan's book *Emperor of the North: Sir George Simpson and the Remarkable Story of the Hudson's Bay* Company (HarperCollins, 2007). In this book, Raffan reports that Simpson stated, "I suspect my name will become as notorious as the late Govr. [William Williams"] in regard to plurality of wives." He also reports that "Simpson's appetite for sex was eclipsed only by his appetite for business, perhaps one tied to the other."

One Pound One, Big Mountain, and Iron Shirt: One Pound One, Big Mountain, and Iron Shirt were Chief Factor Rowand's nicknames.

The wire: Victoria Belcourt Callihoo was the great-granddaughter of Chief Factor Rowand and Lisette Umfreville.

Is la bang le pain?: "La bang" comes from the French beignet (which sounds like bang). A beignet is fried dough, pretty much like donuts or fritters. Bannock fit the description for beignes so Métis called them beignes. La beign (or la bang) is simply translated as the bannock. Traditionally on New Year's Day a meatball stew was served with frybread or bannock, and this dish was called "bullets and bangs" from the French, boulet and beignet.

Kinscape: Métis people who are not on a land base have survived through kinship ties to relatives who reconvene yearly at sites like Lac Ste. Anne Pilgrimage, located near Edmonton, Alberta.

TEXTS CONSULTED

Carter, Sarah and Patricia A. McCormack. *Recollecting: Lives of Aboriginal Women of the Canadian Northwest and Borderlands*. Edmonton: Athabasca University Press, 2011.

Devine, Heather. *The People Who Own Themselves: Aboriginal Ethnogenesis in a Canadian Family, 1660-1900*. Calgary: University of Calgary Press. 2004.

Dobbin, Murray. *The One-And-A-Half Men: The Story of Jim Brady and Malcolm Norris, Métis Patriots of the Twentieth Century*. Regina: Gabriel Dumont Institute of Native Studies and Applied Research, 1981.

Goyette, Linda and Carolina Jakeway Roemmich. *Edmonton: In Our Own Words*. Edmonton: University of Alberta Press, 2004.

King, D.R. *Alberta Archaeology: A Handbook for Amateurs*. High River, Alberta: The High River Times, 1968.

MacGregor, James Grierson. *John Rowand: Czar of the Prairies*. Saskatchewan: Western Producer Prairie Books, 1978.

Macpherson, Elizabeth. *The Sun Traveller: The Story of the Callihoos in Alberta*. St. Albert: Musee Heritage Museum, 1998.

Raffan, James. *Emperor of the North: Sir George Simpson and the Remarkable Story of the Hudson's Bay Company*. Toronto: HarperCollins, 2010.

Spry, Irene M. *The Palliser Expedition: The Dramatic Story of Western Canadian Exploration 1857–1860*. Calgary: Fifth House, 1995.

St-Onge, Nicole, Carol Podruchny, and Brenda Macdougall. *Contours of a People: Métis Family, Mobility, and History*. Norman: University of Oklahoma Press, 2012.

Taylor, Cora. *Victoria Callihoo: An Amazing Life*. Edmonton: Eschia Books, 2009.

Teillet, Jean. *The North-West Is Our Mother*. Toronto: HarperCollins, 2019.

Van Kirk, Sylvia. *Many Tender Ties: Women in the Fur-Trade Society, 1670–1870*. Winnipeg: J. Gordon Shillingford Publishing, 1980.

Wolvengrey, Arok. *nēhiyawēwin: itwēwina. Cree: Words. Vol. 1, Cree-English*. Regina: University of Regina Press, 2001.

Wolvengrey, Arok. *nēhiyawēwin: itwēwina. Cree: Words. Vol. 2, English-Cree*. Regina: University of Regina Press, 2001.

GLOSSARY

(Cree does not use capitalization.)

Cree	English
amiskwaciy-wāskahikan	Beaver Hills House (Edmonton)
awāsis	child
awāsisak	children
āniski-ohtāwīmāw	(male) ancestor, forefather
āpihtawikosisān	Métis
āpihtawikosisānak	Métis people
āpihtawikosisāniskwēw	Métis woman
cāpān	great-grandparent and great-grandchild
ēkwa	and
kinanāskomitin	Thank you
kinēhiyawān cī?	Do you speak Cree?
kinikinik	traditional tobacco mixture (a borrowed term)
kisiskāciwani-sīpiy	swift flowing river (North Saskatchewan)
kōhkom	(your) grandmother
maskihkīwāpoy	tea
maskwacīs	Bear Hills
mihcēto-pīkiskwēwak	speak many languages
misāskwatōmina	saskatoon berries
mosōm	grandfather
mosōmipan	deceased grandfather
mōniyās	white man
mōniyāw	white men
nēhiyaw	Cree
nēhiyawiskwēw	Cree woman

nēhiyawēwin	Cree language
nēhiyāwiwin	Creeness, Cree identity
nikāwiy	my mother
nimāmā	my mother
nimosōmipaṇ	deceased grandfather
nipiy	water
nistikwān	my head
nitōn	my mouth
nīsta	me, too
nīsta mīna	me, as well
nōhkom	my grandmother
nōhtāwiy	my father
ohkomimāw	grandmother
otipēyimisow	Métis person; free person
otipēyimisowak	Métis people, those who are free
otipēyimisowiskwēw	Métis woman
pē-mīciso	come and eat
pīhtikwē	come in
pīwāpiskwēyāpiy	wire
tānisi	hello
wāhkōhtowin	kinship
wēwēpison	cradle
wītaskīwin	Peace Hills

ACKNOWLEDGEMENTS

I gratefully acknowledge the support of the Banff Centre for the Arts, Leighton Studios, for time and space to write.

Thank you to Krista Leddy (beaded chickadee) for the beaded cover image, Jean Okimāsis and Arok Wolvengrey for their Cree proofreading, Katherena Vermette for her editing, Alayna Munce for her copy editing, and Marianne Nicholson for the phrase that inspired the title (*The Chief Factor,* 2019).

Many of the poems gathered here were previously published in *Arc, Room, The Goose, Reclamation and Resurgence: The Poetry of Marilyn Dumont* (Wilfred Laurier University Press, 2024), *Allotment Stories: Indigenous Land Relations under Settler Siege* (University of Minnesota Press, 2022), and *Around the Kitchen Table: Métis Aunties' Scholarship* (University of Manitoba Press, 2024).

Marilyn Dumont is a celebrated poet of Métis ancestry. Her first collection of poetry, *A Really Good Brown Girl* (1996), won the 1997 Gerald Lampert Memorial Award from the League of Canadian Poets; it continues to be read and course-adopted across Canada and in the US. Her most recent book, *The Pemmican Eaters* (2015), won the 2016 Writers' Guild of Alberta's Stephan G. Stephansson Award. She has been the writer-in-residence at five Canadian universities and the Edmonton Public Library as well as an advisor in the Aboriginal Emerging Writers Program at the Banff Centre. She is a full professor of Indigenous Literature and Creative Writing at the University of Alberta. She lives in Edmonton, Alberta.